AMERICAN HEROES

Thomas Jefferson

Let Freedom Ring!

AMERICAN HEROES

THOMAS JEFFERSON

Let Freedom Ring!

SNEED B. COLLARD III

Marshall Cavendish
Benchmark
New York

*To Kent Brown, a friend who has helped
many give voice to words and ideas*

Marshall Cavendish Benchmark
99 White Plains Road
Tarrytown, New York 10591
www.marshallcavendish.us

Collard, Sneed B.
Thomas Jefferson : let freedom ring! / by Sneed B. Collard III.
p. cm. — (American heroes)
"A juvenile biography of Thomas Jefferson, our third president"—
Provided by publisher.
Includes bibliographical references and index.
ISBN 978-0-7614-3067-4
1. Jefferson, Thomas, 1743-1826—Juvenile literature.
2. Presidents—United States—Biography—Juvenile literature. I. Title.
E332.79.C64 2009
973.4'6092—dc22
[B]   2008000057

Editor: Joyce Stanton
Publisher: Michelle Bisson
Art Director: Anahid Hamparian
Designer: Anne Scatto
Printed in Malaysia
1 3 5 6 4 2

Images provided by Debbie Needleman, Picture Researcher, Portsmouth, NH, from the following sources: *Front and back covers*: Bettmann/CORBIS *Pages i, ii, 1, 15, 17, 19, 28:* Bettmann/CORBIS; *pages vi, 11:* The Granger Collection, New York; *page 3:* Special Collections Research Center, Swem Library, College of William and Mary; *page 4:* Emmet Collection, Miriam and Ira D. Wallach Division of Art, Prints and Photographs, The New York Public Library, Astor, Lenox and Tilden Foundations; *page 7:* The New York Public Library/Art Resource, NY; *page 9:* ©Christie's Images Limited; *page 13:* MPI/Getty Images; *page 20:* Pulling Down the Statue of King George III, c. 1859 (oil on canvas) by Johannes Adam Simon Oertel (1823–1909). © Collection of the New-York Historical Society, USA/The Bridgeman Art Library; *page 23:* Gianni Dagli Orti/CORBIS; *pages 25, 31:* Réunion des Musées Nationaux/Art Resource, NY; *page 27:* Image Select/Art Resource, NY; *page 32 left:* Scala/Art Resource, NY; *page 32 right:* CORBIS; *page 34:* Jefferson National Expansion Memorial/National Park Service

CONTENTS

*Thomas Jefferson holds his most famous work,
the Declaration of Independence.*

Th. Jefferson

On March 4, 1801, Thomas Jefferson was sworn in as the third president of the United States. He stood before a crowd of more than one thousand people and began reading his speech. He was so shy and nervous that his voice quivered. Only a few people in the first rows could even hear him! But it was not the power of Thomas Jefferson's voice that was his gift to our nation. It was the power of his words and ideas.

Thomas Jefferson was born on April 13, 1743, in the colony of Virginia. Thomas's mother, Jane Randolph Jefferson, came from a wealthy Virginia family. His father, Peter, owned large pieces of land and was a well-known mapmaker. Peter never got a formal education. But, Thomas later wrote, "He read much and improved himself." Peter Jefferson helped make the first map of Virginia. Thomas was very proud of him.

Thomas's father, Peter Jefferson, helped make the first map of Virginia.

Thomas was born on his family's large country estate, called Shadwell.
There they grew tobacco and had a mill for grinding grain.

The Jeffersons lived on a plantation, a large estate out in the country. Peter Jefferson hired private tutors to make sure that his tall, strawberry-blond son received a strong education. Thomas began his schooling at the age of five. Over time, his hungry mind mastered the English, Latin, Greek, and French languages. Thomas also learned and enjoyed playing the violin.

When Thomas was fourteen, his father died. Peter Jefferson left behind enough money for Thomas to continue his schooling with a tutor, the Reverend James Maury. Thomas soaked up Maury's teaching, but rebelled against the reverend's religious and political views. At age seventeen, Thomas left Maury and entered William and Mary College in Virginia. Here, he met great men of learning. With these men, Thomas spent many happy hours talking about science, philosophy, and the arts. These discussions were Thomas's best education.

At William and Mary College, Thomas got his best education.

Thomas became a lawyer in 1767. But he was more interested in legal ideas than in practicing law. That is not surprising, because trouble was brewing in the American colonies.

During this time, Virginia and the other twelve American colonies were still ruled by the country of Great Britain. Thomas—and most other colonists—felt that even though they lived in America, they should have the same rights as people living in Great Britain. Unfortunately, Britain's King George didn't agree.

Britain's King George did not see eye to eye with Thomas and other Americans.

During the 1760s, the king began charging colonists taxes on tea, paper goods, and other items. The Americans had no say in whether or not they were taxed. Thomas and other patriots wanted Americans to have a voice in the way they were governed. They were very angry at the king. Riots broke out all over the American colonies. Conflict between Great Britain and America grew.

Taxes on tea and other goods led to riots in the American colonies.

Thomas was a natural leader for the colonists. He was educated. He was open to new ideas. He understood government. At the young age of twenty-five, in 1768, he was elected to the Virginia legislature. There he wrote pamphlets and letters urging Great Britain to treat Americans more fairly.

Four years later Thomas fell in love and got married. His bride's name was Martha Wayles Skelton. Both Thomas and Martha had inherited money and land. So, two years after they were married, Thomas closed his law practice. This gave him more time to run his large estate—and join in the conflict with Great Britain.

After Thomas married Martha Wayles Skelton, he closed his law practice. He spent more time working on America's problems with Great Britain.

In 1774, Thomas helped create the Continental Congress. This was a place where leaders from all of the thirteen colonies gathered together to work for the rights of the colonists. King George, though, would not listen to the Americans. In 1775, in the battles of Lexington and Concord, British soldiers and American colonists traded gunfire.

War had begun.

The War for Independence began with the battles of Lexington and Concord, in Massachusetts.

By now, many Americans were determined to create their own country, free from British rule. In the spring of 1776, the men of the Continental Congress decided that America should declare its independence from Great Britain. They chose a committee of five men to write the declaration. It included John Adams, Benjamin Franklin, and, most important, Thomas Jefferson.

*The five committee members at work: From left to right, they are
Benjamin Franklin, Thomas Jefferson (seated in the center),
Robert Livingston (seated at right), John Adams, and Roger Sherman.*

The other members of the committee recognized Thomas's gifts as a writer and thinker. They decided that he would be the best person to write the declaration. So, for the next seventeen days, Thomas locked himself in his room. He poured out his thoughts and his hopes for a new nation, a nation founded on liberty. His words became some of the most important words in the history of the world. They began,

"We hold these truths to be self-evident: that all men are created equal . . ."

Thomas locked himself in his room and poured out his hopes for a new nation.

After the Declaration of Independence was read to the public,
some people in New York City rushed to pull down a statue of King George.

In the Declaration of Independence, Thomas wrote that all men should be treated equally and fairly. He said that every man was born with the right to "Life, Liberty and the pursuit of Happiness." He also wrote that men should be able to choose their own form of government.

It was these ideas, more than any others, that inspired Americans to fight and break away from Great Britain.

It took nearly eight long years, but the colonists finally won their war. They defeated the powerful nation of Great Britain. The United States of America was born!

Thomas Jefferson became the first American ambassador to France. He spent five years in Europe. As an ambassador, he took care of American interests. He also studied plants and farming, architecture and books. He always looked for things that would help Americans build a better, stronger country back home.

Thomas designed the Virginia state capitol after he saw this grand meeting hall in France.

In 1800, Thomas was elected the third president of the United States. One of his biggest accomplishments as president was to buy a huge piece of land from France. The land stretched from Mexico in the south to Canada in the north, and from the Mississippi River in the east to the Rocky Mountains in the west. It was called the Louisiana Purchase, and it doubled the size of our country. To explore this new territory, Thomas launched the Lewis and Clark Expedition. The members of the expedition made maps and collected valuable information about the land and its Native American tribes.

After Thomas completed the Louisiana Purchase, the French flag was lowered and the American flag was raised in the newly acquired territory.

Thomas Jefferson was not perfect. He did not believe that women should be allowed to vote or serve in government. And even though he wrote that all men were created equal, Thomas owned other human beings as slaves.

He and his wife had inherited hundreds of slaves. These slaves worked the Jefferson farmlands and orchards. They labored as servants in the Jefferson house. Slaves were not free. They could be bought and sold like cattle. Thomas knew that this was wrong. During his career, he tried to limit the spread of slavery, but he never did free his own slaves.

Thomas never freed his slaves, although he knew that slavery was wrong.

*Martha Jefferson Randolph was Thomas's eldest child,
and the only one to survive him.*

After completing his second term as president in 1809, Thomas decided to retire from politics. The years had not been easy for him. His wife, Martha, had died only ten years after they were married. Five of their six children would die during Thomas's lifetime. But despite his personal tragedies, Thomas continued to serve his country.

Thomas did more than anyone to create the nation's first public university, the University of Virginia. During the War of 1812, after the British burned the main government library, Thomas sold his own book collection to the nation. This collection would become the Library of Congress.

During his remaining years, Thomas enjoyed making his home, Monticello, more beautiful and comfortable. He continued to read every book he could find. Like Benjamin Franklin, Thomas had a great mind for inventions. He designed a new plow to improve farming on hillsides. He even invented his own machine to make macaroni!

None of this, however, freed him from troubles. Money problems weighed on him. He also worried about the nation he had helped to create. Slavery was an issue with which he—and the rest of the country—never could make peace. He predicted, correctly, that one day slavery would tear our country apart.

During his later years, Thomas spent a lot of time and money improving his beautiful home, Monticello.

No one knew Thomas Jefferson well, but his words continue to inspire us almost two hundred years after his death.

When Thomas Jefferson died on July 4, 1826, no one could claim to have known him very well. As in childhood, many of his thoughts and feelings remained mysterious. Even his friend John Adams wrote that Thomas Jefferson was a "shadow man. His character was like the great rivers whose bottoms we cannot see and make no noise."

But "shadow man" or not, Thomas Jefferson helped our nation shine brightly to the rest of the world. Even today, his words and ideas help guide our country through hard times. They provide hope to all people, everywhere, who dream about freedom and equality.

IMPORTANT DATES

1743 Born on April 13 in Albemarle County in the colony of Virginia.

1767 Begins practicing law.

1768 Elected to Virginia's legislature.

1772 Marries Martha Wayles Skelton.

1774 Retires from the law to run his estate.

1774 Helps call for a Continental Congress to promote the colonies' interests.

1776 Writes the first draft of the Declaration of Independence.

1782 Wife, Martha, dies after childbirth.

1785 Named the first U.S. ambassador to France.

1789 Becomes the nation's first secretary of state.

1796 Elected vice president under President John Adams.

1801 Elected third president of the United States.

1803 Completes the Louisiana Purchase, doubling the size of the United States.

1804 Re-elected president.

1825 Opens the University of Virginia, America's first public university.

1826 Dies at Monticello on July 4, aged 83.

Words to Know

ambassador A person who represents his or her government in a foreign country.

capitol The building in which a state's lawmakers meet.

colonist A person who lives in a colony.

colony A place or territory that is ruled by another country. The people living in a colony have close ties to their "parent" nation but are often not treated as equals by that nation.

Declaration of Independence The famous document that proclaimed that the American colonies were independent from Great Britain.

expedition A journey of discovery or exploration.

independence Freedom from the control of others.

legislature A group of elected people who make laws and help govern a colony, state, or country.

Library of Congress The greatest research library in the United States. Scholars from all over the world come to study at the library.

patriot Someone who loves his or her country and defends or supports it. In Thomas's time, people who supported breaking away from Great Britain were called patriots.

plantation A large estate or farm worked by laborers who live there. The Jefferson plantation, like others in the South in Thomas's day, were worked by African-American slaves.

reverend A person who is authorized by a Christian church to conduct religious ceremonies.

taxes Extra fees on items or services. Governments often raise money by charging people taxes on goods they buy, money they earn, or property they own.

TO LEARN MORE ABOUT THOMAS JEFFERSON

WEB SITES

White House Site
http://www.whitehouse.gov/history/presidents/tj3.html

Library of Congress Exhibit
http://www.loc.gov/exhibits/jefferson/

Thomas Jefferson Monticello Site
http://www.monticello.org/

BOOKS

Don't Know Much about Thomas Jefferson, Vol. 5, by Kenneth C. Davis. HarperCollins Publishers, 2005.

Who Was Thomas Jefferson? by Dennis Brindell Fradin. Penguin Young Readers Group, 2003.

Thomas Jefferson: A Picture Book Biography by James Cross Giblin. Scholastic Publishing, 1994.

Thomas Jefferson by Cheryl Harness. National Geographic Society, 2004.

And for older readers . . .

Give Me Liberty! The Story of the Declaration of Independence by
Russell Freedman. Holiday House, 2000.

PLACES TO VISIT

The Jefferson Memorial
East Basin Drive, SW
Washington, DC
PHONE: (202) 426-6841
WEB SITE: **www.nps.gov/archive/thje/memorial/memorial.htm**

Monticello
931 Thomas Jefferson Parkway
Charlottesville, VA 22902
PHONE: (434) 984-9822
WEB SITE: **www.monticello.org/**

The University of Virginia
Charlottesville, VA
PHONE: (434) 924-0311
WEB SITE: **http://www.virginia.edu/academicalvillage/**

INDEX

Page numbers for illustrations are in boldface.

ABOUT THE AUTHOR

SNEED B. COLLARD III is the author of more than fifty award-winning books for young people, including *Science Warriors*; *Wings*; *Pocket Babies*; and the four-book SCIENCE ADVENTURES series for Benchmark Books. In addition to his writing, Sneed is a popular speaker and presents widely to students, teachers, and the general public. In 2006, he was selected as the *Washington Post*–Children's Book Guild Nonfiction Award winner for his achievements in children's writing. He is also the author of several novels for young adults, including *Dog Sense* and *Flash Point*. To learn more about Sneed, visit his Web site at www.sneedbcollardiii.com.